Table of Contents

Contents

Jan 1, 2014 – Matthew William Ready becomes an East Jefferson County Public Hospital District Commissioner

Unofficial Transcripts from Jefferson Healthcare in Port Townsend, Washington Regular and Special Sessions 2014 - Present

Jan 1, 2014 - Several Meetings between Jan 1 and March 19, 2014 – No audio recording available of dialogue.

March 3, 2014 Jefferson Healthcare Commission Meeting Transcript of Dialogue

Marie Dressler: ...Calling the meeting to order at 3:33. This is Jefferson County Public Hospital District N.2, Board of Commissioners meeting and Commissioner Jill Buhler is excused. Could I ask you what is in front of you? Are you recording this meeting?

Matt Ready: Yes. I'm making an audio recording of this meeting to help me remember what has happened.

Marie Dressler: Okay. Actually that sounds like a good opening for discussion about doing something like that with one of the concerns with the Public Meetings Act as it is being recorded and the Public Hospital District is responsible for safekeeping and so it can all be accessed, maybe this is something that you ought to step in [unclear 00:00:55].

Mike Glenn: Yeah. I think that -- I believe there was going to be a discussion at tonight's meeting about recording board meetings, which I think is a reasonable thing to discuss. There are implications associated with recording board meetings that recording become part of the record and is also part of the Open Public Meeting Act and Records Act, so a recording provided by a hospital, a hospital recording for the purpose of records has to be disclosed when requested and any recording by a board member, according to Council, would be considered that official record. So I think what the discussion tonight was going to go along the lines of discussing it at the board level and then if the board is interested in pursuing that to direct administration to develop a policy, a procedure, and a methodology to make sure that we do it correctly we -- it's in line with our Record Retention Act and Open Public Meeting response team and we do it right. So I think the recommendation from Council is that [if] absent of the hospital doing it, that a board member should not.

Matt Ready: Well, based on my research I don't think that's accurate. I mean, this is a public meeting, citizens have a certain right to record these meetings; I don't surrender that right because I'm a Commissioner, just like we each have the right to vote, you know, we have certain rights, the right to breathe, the right to take notes, I don't think it's -- I would disagree with that assessment of what is legal, or that this constitutes a board act, this is an act as a private citizen.

Mike Glenn: Well, it might be an act of a private citizen but because of your -- because you're a board member, just like the notes you take at a board meeting, they are subject to the Open Public --

Matt Ready: Sure.

Mike Glenn: -- Record Act, so that any tape that you record is also subject to that act, so it becomes part of the record and it's the recommendation from Council looking after the interests of the organization that if Jefferson Healthcare begins to record our meetings, that it be done though Administration so that we have the tape, we have the record, we can properly store it, and we can respond to any open public meeting requests that may come down the pipe, 'cos it's a big thing. Some hospitals do indeed record their meetings and it adds another layer of complexity to responding to open public record requests. So I think [the ask] -- I think the discussion with the rest of the board is, is this something that we want to pursue? And then secondly, if we are going to do it, to do it right and [counsel] -- I don't think anyone is suggesting, as an individual citizen, you don't have the right to make the recording, but as a board member, Council for Jefferson Healthcare is recommending you don't, in the interest of the organization and all of the implications.

Matt Ready: Is the Council recommending me not record meetings?

Mike Glenn: Until we have a policy and a procedure to make sure we can manage that recording in compliance with the Open Public Record Act, that we don't do it, because it's discretionary. Organizations don't have to do it, and further, what I think was going to happen Matt, was that there was going to be a discussion with the other members of the board, should decide if that indeed is the direction that they were going to give Administration.

Matt Ready: I appreciate the recommendation of Council, but I'm going to continue recording the meeting. I think it's a perfectly appropriate decision and I would completely support the board if we wanted to officially do it and I'm happy to give, if you feel like you need a copy to store for seven years, I'm happy to provide that.

Mike Glenn: Well, it's not like I feel like it. The law would require it, and the recommendation from Council is that if a recording is made on behalf of the organization and as a Commissioner you would be making it on behalf of the organization, that we have our own recording.

Marie Dressler: So I will recess this board meeting at 3:39 to see if we can locate a recording -- some recording device, and if not we will just have to [schedule] a special meeting. Thank you.

[Pause]

Marie Dressler: [Inaudible] At 3:43 I will reconvene the meeting [inaudible] Hospital District N. 2, I continue our meeting.

Tony Deleo: Madam Chairman, if you would [unclear 00:07:05] that Commissioner Ready is no longer recording the meeting.

[00:10:46]

Hilary Whittington: Today we'll be talking through the January finance report and then a preview for February. It has been a tricky couple of months, and while circumstances that should never affect the timeliness of the reports, running a hospital without a controller has certainly changed my life a bit, so at this point we are - we didn't have the income statement for February complete today, so we'll be talking through January and we'll have the February report shortly...

...In general, we were where we needed to be from a revenue standpoint knowing that we have not yet acquired the Port Townsend Surgical Associate's Practice, and that is a lot of the difference that we'll see on the income side.

...At the last meeting, we looked at the departments where we were over and under budget, so I didn't want to repeat that, but for the month we landed about $280 thousand under our budget and our revenue adjustments were in line with that.

...In general, the profit can be somewhere in the $60 to $100 thousand range per month. If we billed that at the high end of our budget we could be overstating our budget by a million dollars per year; that's not somewhere that we wanted to go as a leadership team. So we will expect that, based on the month, this may or may not be over budget, but know that we took a conservative approach in our budgeting efforts somewhat intentionally.

...So days of cash: in the next few slides we talked about at the last meeting, the last finance presentation. We landed January with 44 days of cash and that equated to about 8.3 million in cash. At this point, we are a bit above, I took the cash balances just a couple of days ago and we're at about 8.5 million. That keeps us, since our expenses were higher since the beginning of the year, that keeps our days in cash about where they have been for the last couple of months. This just excludes the third party settlements, and at this point there are no incredibly large third party settlements out there.

Our days in A/R: our days in A/R at this point, as of this morning, is actually 84, and I know that for the last couple of months I've been sitting here and telling you that our days will be going down. A couple of drivers [unclear 00:21:05] and I want to be very transparent about where those drivers come from and what our plan is to fix them. So as revenues go up, our days in AR also go up. Days in accounts receivable is a direct calculation of taking all of the revenue and considering how much we earn per day and then looking at our accounts receivable, so as revenue changes, so do our days in accounts receivable. Also there have been some delays. There's a system called FIS and this system actually has a gigantic impact on our days in accounts receivable. It's where the Medicare payments flow through. So there was a glitch in FIS in the first week of March, which caused a week pause in the FIS system. So knowing that that happened, it kind of delayed all of those collections for the hospital by one week, so that gained three days of accounts receivable right there. In the last couple of weeks my entire dedication, aside from the audit, has been on reducing days in accounts receivable and we are working with a couple of vendors to figure out how we can get the backlog taken care of.

The issue is that the backlog that happened when we went live with Epic is considerable and while we can stay on top of all of the claims that we are receiving and keep our days in A/R consistent, working a backlog of essentially 30 days of accounts receivable is a difficult task. So we are coming up with a work plan to figure out whether it is additional employee time or working with vendors on our older accounts receivable from our commercial carriers or Medicare, to try and just work through the old things.

Matt Ready: So I assume the countermeasures for increasing cash on hand and catching up on accounts receivable are the same as at the previous meeting.

Hilary Whittington: They are.

Marie Dressler: Work in progress.

Hilary Whittington: Work in progress. Yes.

Matt Ready: So we should note that cash on hands and a number of days of accounts receivable is still not at the board documented target and I recommend approving --

Marie Dressler: Well, we don't have to approve anything, because we've already had the financial report.

Matt Ready: It's not a financial monitoring report?

Hilary Whittington: Yes, actually --

Marie Dressler: Yes, but it's not the annual, it's not annual, which is what I believe we were -- it's just a report we are presented with, I don't know that we necessarily have to approve it. We haven't been, as you're well aware, we haven't been following the [unclear 00:32:37] governance strictly, and that's why we're having a workshop in April to review all this, because some things we modified it prior to you coming on to the board and so there's no reason reviewing and reevaluating how we use the governance, as you're well aware of it.

Matt Ready: I was just going by the board policy that says we monitor those two items and monthly we get the financial flash report. I assume we --

Marie Dressler: What I'm saying to you is we've not been following that, as you're well aware, and that's come up and that's why we're having a two-day workshop. I appreciate your point. Thank you.

Matt Ready: So, are we not approving any monitoring reports at all at any monthly board meeting?

Marie Dressler: I don't think we need to, unless it's something that the other board members I mean just jump in.

Chuck Russell: Well, we haven't been --

Marie Dressler: We haven't been, yeah.

Chuck Russell: -- our governance policies aren't something that was brought down to us from the State or from anybody else. It's something we imposed on ourselves, and they're in a state of flux right at the moment. We've scheduled meetings to "unflux" them.

Marie Dressler: [Laughs] Is that in the dictionary?

Tony Deleo: I'm sure it is.

Hilary Whittington: Matt, just one comment to you is these reports I presented the targets that you're talking about, those were presented in February, so those -- the slides I think were recognized as monitoring reports or however it was titled, but the information that I shared today, those few slides were -- they [weren't] different.

Matt Ready: Okay, but I'm hearing we're never going to -- or at least until we decide we're not currently approving monitoring reports.

Marie Dressler: That is my understanding from what was agreed prior to you coming on the board, and then we sort of -- we've "toed" and "froed" and so that's why general consensus was we need to get this sorted out and we have two meetings, as you know, in April or at least they're planned for April, where we will with someone who is trained in governance will help us decide as a board where we're going with this.

Matt Ready: Joyce, do you know how we compare to the median of comparable institutions with patient satisfaction?

Joyce: I do, and I -- you know, hospital compare I presented that, I can't remember what meeting it was in, but I presented it in a previous board meeting and on the hospital compare website you can pick out different hospitals that you want to compare yourself to. So I always compare us to Harrison and Olympic because they're the closest to us, and we have been consistently much higher than they have been in almost every score. However, I don't know what will happen when this data hits because that data is always several quarters behind. On our picker we can get our peer ranking, we can get it for small hospitals, and we can get it for the whole picker data base, and I don't think that quarter is not -- I have to click on it to give that -- but I can provide that information, I'd be happy to.

[01:38:45]

Tony Deleo: If the board is amiable to it, I'd like to make a motion that by resolution we request the Attorney General's Office to have the supply to all elected officials in the State of Washington.

Matt Ready: I'd second that.

Matt Ready: So I have a few items for board business. I've been thinking a lot about healthcare affordability and I have a couple -- I have two proposals that I'd like to share with my fellow Commissioners and I've been working on these for quite a while. I know this is your first pass in hearing them, so I imagine you may not have a lot of comments today, but I'm hoping we will get a chance to discuss them in detail perhaps at our next regular session.

The first one is defining board expectations for collections, practices, and policies. Now, the board has defined and often talked about what our expectations are for how the public hospital district conducts medical care, but I don't believe we've given really clear documented guidance regarding our expectations of financial services and how they interact with our patients. I think it would be helpful, moving forward, if we add to our ends goals policy a clear statement characterizing our expectations for how the Hospital District financially impacts lives of patients and families, so what I propose is that we add to our ends policy the Jefferson Healthcare billing charity care and collections policies and practices will be fair, reasonable, and as compassionate as possible within the limits of the law and available resources. If we like that and we agree to that, we could then discuss how we might monitor something like that, and that's sort of modeled after some other similar sort of statements I found at other institutions. Unless there are any comments, I will go straight to the next --

Marie Dressler: Well, I was just thinking that this sort of thing would come up when we're doing the review of our governance.

Matt Ready: Yeah, that would be great.

Marie Dressler: That would be an appropriate time to -- yeah, perfect. Also, you know, Miss Buhler should be back then and so it'll be a full board. I think it's not a bad idea at all.

Matt Ready: Yeah.

Tony Deleo: Madam Chairman, I also like to suggest in things like this that apparently are going to be in depth, that possibly we get the material printed in advance so you look at it and put some thought it in before we --

Matt Ready: Sure.

Marie Dressler: Yes, you're not going to get any comments back today --

Matt Ready: So is it just as simple as saying, "I'd like 10 minutes on the agenda to talk about two proposals I've drafted"?

Marie Dressler: Well, I think taking from what Tony just said is that bring with you some information or even I guess ahead of time --

Tony Deleo: I prefer in advance to have some time to look at it.

Marie Dressler: -- and so that we've got some time to look at it and know, you know, so we can think about it --

Matt Ready: Sure.

Marie Dressler: -- because it might not be something that we have particularly thought, put a lot of detailed thought into it --

Matt Ready: Yeah, I could just email to everyone one way as long as we don't discuss it over the email [crosstalk]

Marie Dressler: Yeah, to the board, and we don't expect to reply to it either, you know, so...

Matt Ready: Yeah.

Chuck Russell: You said these were modeled on other -- could you include those other institutions?

Tony Deleo: Yeah, the references.

Marie Dressler: Yeah, the re- yeah, include references like you would normally in anything like this.

Matt Ready: Sure, yeah. Okay.

Marie Dressler: That sounds good.

Matt Ready: I would like to read the second proposal. The second proposal is that the board consider monitoring the use of third party collection agencies by the Hospital District. A collection's monitoring report would help us monitor several board policy goals, including those in finance, patient satisfaction, public image and community health. I know our financial counselors work really hard with patients to come up with affordable solutions, but I believe some it does not work, and it doesn't work out for our patients, and when that happens, sometimes patients are sent to collections with a medical debt they cannot afford, and if this ever happens, the consequences are severe.

These consequences include a patient's credit getting damaged, a patient potentially being subjected to extraordinary collection actions in the name of Jefferson Healthcare but being done by separate agencies, it doesn't have the direct oversight of Jefferson Healthcare staff, patients may learn to view Jefferson Healthcare as an adversary rather than as a partner and steward in the healthcare of the community, and the patient may learn that seeking healthcare will severely negatively impact them financially, and so they stop seeking it properly when needed, putting their future health at risk, contributing to the likely hood of preventable emergency care in the future, and if that patient does have to get emergency care in the future they probably won't be able to afford it, and the public ends up paying for it anyways.

I know you're all familiar with that story in healthcare, and I know all my fellow Commissioners want Jefferson Healthcare to be a partner and steward of the health of our community, and I think monitoring how much we're making use of collections agencies will give us a valuable perspective in how well we're working towards that goal. I know we have a fiduciary responsibility to collect on debts, but I also recognize that the mission of this organization is not to maximize profits at the expense of health, the health of our community. I know none of us want to do that. We want to be compassionate partners in the health of our community and this means we have to be I think really mindful of anything we're doing that may in fact harm people, and collections is a pretty -- it can be a harmful thing, so I just think we really need to watch it carefully. So due to the great potential consequences in the realms of finance, customer satisfaction, community health, and public image that result when sending a patient to collections, I propose we start monitoring this. We could start with simply a study of collections activities at

Jefferson Healthcare that would include things like trends and totals for the total number of accounts that are currently held by a third party collection agency, the monthly number and percent of patients that are sent to collections, total money that we recover through this effort, total money written off because it does not succeed through collections, and maybe annual data. Then, if we look at this data maybe we will see some opportunity to set goals or guidelines for the institution. So I know that's a lot of information and I really appreciate the desire to have gotten ahead of time and so I'll just email you guys copies of what I just shared, and I'd love to discuss it at some point in the future.

Marie Dressler: Thanks so much. Great. Do you have anything?

Chuck Russell: No.

Marie Dressler: Okay.

Matt Ready: I have one more thing. The last meeting, I asked if there was interest in publishing our bylaws and policies online. There was some thought that you would like to think about it. I'm wondering if anyone is interested in discussing putting our board policies and bylaws online.

Marie Dressler: I think this will come again at the April -- because we don't have anything we're going to put up at the moment, because we're going through reviews and revisions and decision as to what form of governance -- that's my personal take on it, so I don't know what --

Tony Deleo: I believe I recommended the last meeting that we wait publishing that until we have the final out of our rewrite. I think publishing one and then a month later publishing a second one could be confusing.

Marie Dressler: Yeah. Do you have any comment, Chuck?

Chuck Russell: No. I agree with Tony. I think I -- what we talked about.

Matt Ready: I mean personally I think there are current policies, and I think it's reasonable to put the current policies that we've been operating under up, but I sense I'm not going to get a second to that motion. The last thing is there was a community health need's assessment meeting with the Health Department, received a ton of data on access in our community, lots of great information that we are sifting through, and there's one more big data meeting that's going to go over mental health and chemical dependency information in our community.

Marie Dressler: Good. That's good.

Tony Deleo: At what time would we expect to see the report?

Matt Ready: I don't know what the timeline is. There's no way of -- we have a meeting in the next month and then they have to start -- we have to start sifting through it and pair it down. Hopefully within two months.

Tony Deleo: Would you give us a timeline when you have something?

Matt Ready: Yeah.

Tony Deleo: So we can work around that.

Matt Ready: Yeah.

Tony Deleo: It would be a valuable tool I think and [look if they need to, our community]. Possibly that fulfills some of our requirements [unclear 01:48:27] critical access hospitals as far as the assessment [unclear 01:48:30] who does it.

Mike Glenn: That's not a requirement. I just think it a good idea.

Marie Dressler: That's it, Matt?

Matt Ready: Yeah.

March 2015 - Numerous Meetings between March 3, 2014 and June 24, 2015 – Audio available but not yet transcribed.
June 24, 2015 - Jefferson Healthcare Commission Meeting in Chelan, Wa Transcript of Dialogue

Jill Buhler: [00:00:00] ...Session meeting of June 24, 2015, in Chelan, Washington. The order of business --

Tony Deleo: [00:00:12] And officially recorded.

Marie Dressler: [00:00:15] By Commissioner Ready.

Jill Buhler: [00:00:16] And it's being recorded by Commissioner Ready. The purpose is for review of our governance policies. So basically, what we want to know is what's working and what's not, and what can we do about it.

Matt Ready: [00:00:40] So are we debriefing the conference, or are we talking about our governance policies?

Jill Buhler: [00:00:44] We're talking about governance policies and the conference. Anything we learned in the conference that would be like that.

Tony Deleo: [00:00:52] I'll jump out as far as governance goes. The policy governance concept was a great experiment, in that like some things, like nuclear weapons, don't necessarily end up with what you intended. My take is that I think, in a time of transition, as we're moving from a long time administrator into a new administrator, until we develop the relationship, I think this is probably the transitional tool. I think now we've developed a relationship with Mike, I think the idea of us having him do the busy work of generating reports that are really not the type of reports he normally puts on his desk or on his staff's desks, with us giving him in effect a moving target, saying, "Create the report," he does and we say, "It's not quite right, try again," to me it is not work.

The communication we want is more collegial, not if you will, him be a talking head and we sit in the audience and watch. I'd like to see more of a conversation, more -- you know, what's really on the radar right now and what's doing great? More of a dashboard type of thing. I'm just going to speak for me. I really appreciate seeing all the C-Suite every meeting, but something in my gut tells me that all these people have way more important things to do then to sit and smile at us. I mean, this is your take -- this is yours Mike, this is your people, but I think just whatever reports like you make for fiscal, is just -- give us copies, email it to us and maybe, whether one or two paragraphs summary cover sheet, and let us go through it. If we have any questions, we'll call you. And just quit making busy work for people who already have too much stuff to do that's more important. That's just my take.

Chuck Russell: [00:03:11] Well, I think one of the reasons that we were experimenting with I guess, as you know it, policy governance, was to prevent micromanagement by Commissioners, [different questions of the] hospital, and I think we succeeded in doing that at some extent, and we've seen other government entities fall prey to that micromanagement setup. County Commissioners used to do it pretty badly. I think they're getting better at it, but would we fall back into a micromanagement type situation if we abandon policy government? Any opinions?

Marie Dressler: [00:03:59] Well, I came onto the board after this was a done deal. I understood why it was done in the first place, but it seems to me very cumbersome. It's designed for corporate private businesses as opposed to public hospital districts or any other public entity, and I think it's very cumbersome, and I don't know that it serves any particular purpose. Our role is represented of the entire community, our roles, and we need to know from a level of governance, as opposed to operations, what is going on, because we hire somebody who hires a team to run the hospital district on behalf of us, the representers of the community, and I just see it as very cumbersome and --

[Door opens]

Marie Dressler: -- I see it as very cumbersome and not productive and quite a time waster. I also do have concerns about interference or Commissioners getting into operations, which is not what we were elected to do. So I don't know exactly to create a better balance, but that's where I'm coming from with it.

Tony Deleo: [00:05:51] Speaking for myself, being the most senior person having been there forever, is that part of the benefit of the policy governance was the transition for me from a time with [Vic] when we basically all sat around the table and run the place. I mean not by choice but just by necessity --

Chuck Russell: [00:06:12] Somebody had to do it.

Tony Deleo: [00:06:13] Yeah. Well, from just a lack of support, C-Suite, I mean we had a CFO, a CNO and [Vic].

Marie Dressler: [00:06:21] Well, that's right. When I used to go to meetings back in the '80s, that's how it was.

Tony Deleo: [00:06:25] Yeah, and the policy governance I think has broken the old habits to the extent, and I really do feel that we should be able to release ourselves, if somebody's playing in somebody else's sandbox I think we can wheel each other back in, I would hope anyway, help where to a level of collegial monitoring that we can deal without.

Chuck Russell: [00:07:00] But policy governance was created or adopted by us to solve the problem that we had, and I think it kind of did and I don't think we'd drop back into that but we might. One of the things that is helpful aside of that is the Patient Advocate Office, which solves a lot of that because when we used to have a constituent come to us with a problem, we didn't know what else to do except go try to solve the problem with management. It's much better now to run it through the Patient Advocate Office.

Mike Glenn: [00:07:38] Yeah. That's the place to go.

Tony Deleo: [00:07:42] The systems are in place to assure all of us that the organization's being run incredibly well, and to just keep us informed of where it's going, what the issues are, how we can help resolve them, and basically, you know, get us the hell out of the road so you can do your job.

Marie Dressler: [00:08:07] Well, I think that's how we have to judge it, it's just how well it is running, you know, how patients have access to care, how the departments are running, how we're either getting dinged by auditors or any of the other entities who audit us, as [DNV] or our accreditations and certifications. So if those outside entities in their evaluations are of a sufficiently high standard, then that has I think a way of evaluating how things are being run and also with input from constituents, who are very free with their comments and hopefully -- and then getting reports from time to time, like patient advocates, like the financial situation.

Jill Buhler: [00:09:12] What if we asked administrators what -- Mike to come up with a list of what he feels are good indicators of how the operation's working, what would be the best measuring devices, best measuring aspects of that, because the way I see it, none of us board members is an expert in this. We all have our own perspective, and that's good, that's why there's five of us, that's why we're not all from the same ilk is because we can ask different questions from different perspectives and I think that's a -- but none of us have the expertise that Mike does. So why are we trying to second-guess? We have the most valuable tool right here, and that's our CEO. So I believe we need to ask that input, that's who we need to rely on. If the CEO, and I'm not talking about Mike one bit, but if the CEO is not performing, then that's what we deal with, is getting a new CEO. Otherwise, I think we need to listen to the CEO, work in collaboration with the CEO, and find out -- work together as a team, because that's -- one without the other is of no benefit.

Chuck Russell: [00:10:56] And policy governance was giving us sort of a tool to judge the CEO, but it was pretty darn cumbersome. I think we all should give ourselves more credit for having enough sense to be able to do it ourselves.

Tony Deleo: [00:11:10] In some ways it almost created a barrier, you know, this is Mike, this is us, and we can't really talk to some extent; here's the report we want, you make a report, okay, that works, and that's the end of the communications. It's not real dialogue, that I'd like to have.

Mike Glenn: [00:11:32] I have kind of two issues with policy governance, as it's defined. The first is, there is supposed to be this deep and wide crocodile-filled moat separating governance from operations, and when I first got here I was so accustomed to budget committees and quality committees and what I recall, we need a bridge, bridge the moat, that policy governance [grooves be damned]. I really think we need to bridge the moat, so that there can be discussion about affiliation and those sort of things, so that there is some dialogue and then you would have to manage, you know, where does governance stop and operations begin, but I think if everybody was committed to align, separating the two, we could work that out.

The second issue that I had is the monitoring records that when I first got here, I think it's fair to say that the organization was underperforming, but we were all green on our monitoring reports, and so I paid no attention to those and [unclear 00:13:00] on here are the things that I think need to occur to make this hospital run better and the healthcare system run better. So fast forward to today, I think that there's -- the monitoring reports are better but they're still, you know, we could hit all green on those monitoring reports but the organization could go to hell.

What I have seen work well is a scorecard that spans the balance scorecard, where here's the patient safety and quality, and here's our financial, and our productivity, and engagement, and we just sort of provide reports on all of that but in a less -- the structure is that there are organizational scorecards and CEO scorecards. So the structure that, you know, if we're doing things we say we're going to do, then that would influence your evaluation of the CEO, but it wouldn't be this exercise of, do you accept the report in which, from our perspective seems clunky, particularly the exercise a couple of years ago when because of [Vic], our days and cash were or weren't where it was and we had to go through this process of pointing out that we're below [unclear 00:14:40] and that just sort of sent this ripple through all the people working on that, that we would have preferred not to have them sent. And it really didn't add an ounce of value if Hilary [didn't lead those meetings], go working harder, or wow, we're not meeting this metric, let's go work on it. And we probably had more anxiety about what the organization would look like at the end of the year if cash was forty days, then I would [unclear 00:15:12].

So I think that somewhere in the middle and we cold -- 'cos the board ultimately owns what those indicators are, but if they start from us, you know, years of stuff we watch, that we talk about it as [LG] mostly motivated our influence by things that are -- that we need to do well to meet needs or what's coming around the corner, then the board could say, "Yes, this is the report card at the end of the year," and that would be the report card for 2016, and we could set up some sort of reporting mechanism but the reports for things that we're working on come easy. A quality report, Joyce pulls that together in an hour because it's all the stuff that we are continuously working on; Hilary's report, all of these metrics and all of these things that we are continuing trying to improve or understand. So I think that that would, from our perspective, would be more tightly aligned with green on the report card and the likelihood the organization is doing well, and I think be a more productive and meaningful use of our time. But I guess I'll stop right in it, the year report I think that we can contribute to them but ultimately you guys have to like say, "Yeah, that is what we want to judge the performance of the organization and of the CEO based on these things," also integrate this strategic plan into that too.

Chuck Russell: [00:17:19] We really have given it a good try. We've spent god knows how many hours trying to make it work.

Jill Buhler: [00:17:27] Well, we knew going in that it wasn't designed for a public hospital district. It was a corporate tool, and we said we would modify it and we have, but question might be the modifications of where we're working.

Chuck Russell: [00:17:45] But if we dump it, do we need to replace it?

Jill Buhler: [00:17:47] Well, we do. We have to have some form.

Chuck Russell: [00:17:51] Yeah.

Jill Buhler: [00:17:51] Some agreement.

Tony Deleo: [00:17:53] I think it's something that Mike and us can work on. Something that works for both of us, and I would hope that we have a strong enough relationship between the board and Mike [unclear 00:18:06] gain the information will call to him, "Mike, I'd like to know about this." On the other side, if one of us is sticking our nose in the wrong door, he'd feel comfortable slamming it on us. I mean, that's the kind of work relationship I'd like between you and the board. That's where it should be. We should all be around the table able to speak our minds.

Jill Buhler: [00:18:33] So do we keep some of the policies and not the others? Or do we discard the whole thing? Or do we what? Matt, you're not -- what do you think?

Matt Ready: [00:18:43] I don't think we ever fully implemented policy governance. I think the moment our consultant left us our pace of successfully working through how policy governance worked, dragged to a complete six-month painful slide, but I don't think we ever got to a place where you're supposed to get where the board goes through a rigorous process defining the purpose and ends goal of the hospital. We defined -- we did good work to get what we got, which was four bullet points, very high level, but we did not do the work it takes to actually get to clear measurable metrics for, this is what we want you to accomplish Mike or CEO.

And I also agree, we didn't get a point where we were monitoring the right stuff. We never fully implemented monitoring reports, so we never were actually doing the monitoring part I think in the rigorous way that you're supposed to do it with policy governance, and I totally agree with your sentiment; we need to monitor the right stuff. I think that's a problem that can be solved in policy governance. If you're monitoring the wrong stuff, you've got to figure out, how do you fix that? and I go back to Sherry Jennings. What she said when I asked her during our meeting, "What are the other styles of governance that you think work well? and she said, "There aren't other styles of board governance." This is the only effective model of board governance that she knows of. So without an effective board governance model, what you have is a board that either is often doing stuff it shouldn't be doing, which can be a problem, or it's basically largely *heavily* heavily reliant on just trusting the CEO absolutely knows what he's doing, absolutely knows what are the right goals, the right indicators, the right mission of the hospital, and you just basically do what you were saying, you're just trusting that your CEO will always come up with the right strategic plan, 'cos there's nothing to compare it to.

If the board doesn't have clear ends, and clear goals that is driving the CEO how he's forming his strategic plan, then he's presenting a strategic plan and then everyone is sort of saying, "Does that feel right to me? Does that feel like we're missing something?" And I'm not saying -- I mean of course we have to trust our CEO's expertise, but it's our job to govern and it is our job to second-guess our CEO. It's our job and we never follow the part of policy governance that says the board's job is to be studying big trends, studying what is going on in our community, studying having people come in to present presentations about big things that are happening that might affect your business and you're supposed to be thinking about that as you're crafting your ends structure, and as you're guiding your CEO.

We never changed our agenda; our agenda has stayed pretty much the exact same way it's been. The agenda of a policy governance board is different. It's supposed to be a different type of meeting, more efficient, more substantive --

Marie Dressler: [00:22:37] Can I ask you a question Matt on that? In comparing it to, say a corporation which is a private corporation or private hospital that uses governance, how many times a month or a year do those boards meet?

[Crosstalk] Are they every two weeks or are they…?

Jill Buhler: [00:22:59] I can tell you that policy governance, when the three of us went to the Intensive Care module of it and five days of I mean really intensive work in Atlanta, the whole agenda is nothing but a monitoring report, and that's it . The CEO comes in, gets the monitoring report, we say aye, nay, end of story. That's all.

Tony Deleo: [00:23:30] Then you do the consent agenda and you go home. I mean that's it.

Matt Ready: [00:23:38] I mean I have my book on policy governance, I could read what an agenda of a policy governance means, or we can have -- but I mean, none of us are experts on it. We had an expert that was helpful and so it wasn't just us arguing this is how policy governance works. She was able to intervene in these disagreements and actually give us an answer. But this is what we did for six months when we were trying to work on it, but now we're back to us--none of us being experts in policy governance--arguing over our pictures in our minds of what, you know -- I'm not saying I'm an expert on it, we will have imperfect pictures of it 'cos none of us has actually seen it operate correctly.

Mike Glenn: [Unclear 00:24:18] College implemented policy governance, and once a month they meet and they run under this policy governance guideline, so maybe go to one of those board meetings and what you would find is that they are a lot more like our board meeting than what you may think or what the diagram in Sherry Jennings brochure says they should be like. So that is my other experience with policy governance, and there's a school district outside of Tacoma, so maybe that would be a good exercise rather than reading Carver's book.

Secondly, what I heard from Sherry Jennings is that there are no other canned--and I don't mean that in a pejorative way--governance models, but you suggest that there is no other effective way of governing, I can't accept that. There is probably 37 public hospital districts that would argue, certainly one in Port Angeles would, because they feel very good about their level of governance and I think they do a great job, but there are very few policy governance models in the State of Washington and there are lots of effective governance going on. So Sherry is just like saying there is not -- here are the five models, you know, like football and offensive coordinator, you know, here are the five different ways in which you can setup your offense. Apparently there's only one, the Carver model policy governance of ABCD , but there is effective governance going on and every board has their bylaws and their policy's procedures, and it sort of paints this picture of how they work, and some are very effective. I think some aren't, but I don't think it's an all or nothing. You either embrace policy governance or you are you ineffectual.

Marie Dressler: [00:26:28] That's University Place, this is called District University, Place down near Tacoma that you might want to -- it's all online if you want to look it up.

Jill Buhler: [00:26:39] And the course that we link to is taught by Miriam Carver herself.

Tony Deleo: [00:26:43] Miriam and John, both [crosstalk].

Marie Dressler: [00:26:45] Both of them. So it came right from the horse's mouth.

Tony Deleo: [00:26:50] Well, okay. I'll go with your term.

[Laughs]

Tony Deleo: [00:26:56] We've been to the pope, we've been to the Vatican on policy governance and to me, from doing the homework on it, from going through the program, in a corporate setting it works great. The corporation develops the package, the package gives it to the board president, the board president presents it at the annual board meeting, and every month or every quarter they look at the reports and say, "Okay!" and they pop the corks on the champagne, everybody has, you know, nice social evening, but anywhere you look at a situation like that, you have to depend on the people who are running the show to know what's important, to know where we've got to be going, to know how to get there. You mentioned about we need to do a homework. Well, I don't know about you, but now I do a lot of homework, a lot of webinars, a lot of reading, a lot of research. Yes. [Crosstalk] From the questions I ask her, she'll tell you, and I use that research to be able to see if what Mike is telling us is making sense. If it's following where the industry is going, and it's being right on the mark.

Mike Glenn: [00:28:20] I don't think it's policy governance or lawless, and hope you hired an incredible administrative team, that the other forms of effective governance they've got the boundaries, they've got the bumper guards, they've got the levels of performance, they've got missions and visions and value statements. All of that work can be done within a non-policy governance framework and it should be done. I mean, it doesn't feel like to me, it never has felt like to me in any job that the CEO administration has carte blanche ability to say, let's go off in this direction. What I think needs to feel like, regardless of policy or governance model, is we are all in this together, we've sort of defined who we are, and what we do, and who we do it for, and plan to execute on that. Interestingly, and it's two different perspectives looking at the same thing, it might be possible that you look at the policy governance framework and think that is an enabler to what I've just described, I look at it as a barrier, a clunkier way. It just seems to me that it's kind of a Rube Goldberg barrier-ridden model to try to do the work I'm convinced we all want to do, but it is in no way -- moving away from policy governance isn't shirking accountability. There are non-policy governance models that are created that place a ton of accountability on administration.

Jill Buhler: [00:30:29] And that's the key, it's accountability. That's what governance is about. That's the end result, is every member involved? Being held accountable? Is a board being held accountable for doing its work the way it should? Is the CEO being accountable for doing the work he should? Is the CFO doing…? Etc., all the way down the line. So how we get there is the vehicle that we're looking at, not the destination.

Tony Deleo: [00:31:02] As far as just taking Mike's word for it, that everything is okay, I've got to the point from being with Mike, watching with Mike, that I, who's probably the most cynical person you ever going to walk into, accept what he says, but I also compare that against all the reports we get, out DNV certification, the [unclear 00:31:25], all the reports, the state audits, everything that we get says we're going in the right direction, we're taking care of the people, they're getting out alive, they're getting out happy alive for the most part. I mean we're changing our clinic operations to where they're being more efficient that we can see more people. We've gone out and [beat the brush] to bring people in under the expanded Medicaid Program to not only give them health care but give them some dignity, that they don't have to come to us with open hand and beg for a cherry. I mean our organization has done under Mike and this team's leadership some really incredible stuff, and if you look at pure policy governance, here's what it'd say, you're going to do this, this, and this, and every month he brings us a report and says, "I did it," and we say, "Okay," and we're done. If you want to talk about two systems that are irresponsible on the part of the governing board, that's the one. He presents a report, and if it's within the parameters established, it's okay, we accept it, as opposed to all of us sitting around and saying, "Okay, what's going on?" You're not looking at the numbers, looking at the things that are going on.

Marie Dressler: [00:32:44] And looking at the trends, looking at where we're falling down where we can improve, what we can do.

Tony Deleo: [00:32:49] And where are we going, are our tracks parallel to other successful organizations in healthcare.

Hilary Whittington: [00:32:56] There's an interesting thing from my angle and we present these monitoring reports about finance, but there actually isn't space for us to give you cool information just to go talk about in the community. Yet, we're in a community where your roles are spokespeople for the hospital in a lot of ways, but because we're focused on, here's the monitoring report, here's days in account receivable, you're never going to go brag to the community that we dropped three days in accounts receivable, but if we--

Marie Dressler: [00:33:23] And what would it mean to the community?

Hilary Whittington: [00:33:24] Right. It actually would feel like it's a bad thing collecting faster, it could be that we're pushing out people faster, but I would be excited. I like reports out from different people and this is all just me thinking of what it means to our community or to our hospital folks to know you, to feel they have a connection with the board, and I think that presentations by other folks can be a very valuable way for them to feel like they have a connection to the board and so they know they're giving information to you and that you are helping us share information with the community, that cool things are going on. We don't necessarily know about those a year in advance to give you a monitoring report on compliance or on privacy or quality or whatever those things are, but to our folks, even though it just takes some time, it's an incredible opportunity for them to have a chance to talk to them. So I hope that wherever we land, that even though it does take time for Aaron Brown to create a presentation, that helps us create leaders going forward and I hope that we don't lose that opportunity. Having space for us to share, *here's what's going on*, and right now with the monitoring report you don't get the story, so is hard for you to walk out into the community and share that because you're getting a *we are great*, or *we are above the line that we are supposed to be above*, but [crosstalk] --

Mike Glenn: [00:34:50] Or this is the reports that the calendar says that we need to report on.

Hilary Whittington: [00:34:54] Exactly, and I struggle with that with the patient [unclear 00:34:58] report for sure. I think having the *yes, we're doing this in the correct amount of time*, I don't know if that would be as -- I mean hearing that [unclear 00:35:08] recorder, it's valuable information for sure, but that's not something that you'll remember and talk to your [family at dinner] about. Those are statistics and we're getting above the line in what way are required to do, but the stories that go with it, I mean, a patient's story is what I remember out of the board meetings more than anything else, but if we think the board is -- we're not in Seattle at a gigantic corporation, we're in a space where you're certainly playing a different role in the community than in a larger area where you'd be anonymous.

Tony Deleo: [00:35:42] Hilary, we really appreciate your input about staff interaction with us at the board meetings, because I always had some kind of concern that it was just an exercise just because you were supposed to do it but if it's part of development, if it's of use to you and the team, then I'm all for it continuing that.

Mike Glenn: [00:36:02] Yeah, it's a big deal. I think that we're a public organization, but yet 99 plus percent of our business model is how well we run the operation. So I view, one thing that I use the board meetings for, for at least two reasons; one reason is it's an opportunity, whether there's five people from the public there or two, Roger and Alison, or Charlie and Alison, to talk about positive things that are going on that the community should know about, and speaks to positive and productive things that we are doing.

Secondly, I use it for an opportunity to manage people up. There's a lot of people that are playing these minor roles at Jefferson Healthcare, but doing them superbly. So why are things going better today than they were going, you know, a year ago, two years ago? Because we just have more of those people that are doing better work and doing it in more concert with each other. So some of that is an organization that seems to be doing okay. Kevin is this guy that you've probably seen him at a handful of our meetings, but I don't know what he does, but he is the guy that -- Hilary's and Ted's right hand person that makes the revenue cycle work. The way you all need to think about the revenue cycle is if the revenue cycle works, and the money is flowing, it doesn't become a distraction from all of our other work, and that's the reality. They reality, when you get one day of your expenses covered by taxes, is that you have to sweat the other 364 days, or you can't do even the most fundamental work of running the hospital. You certainly can't do the work that we heard Todd [Linnen] talk about or the other speakers. So Kevin, that's his deal.

Whenever -- there will be some spike where, you know, usually it's a big number, like, what the heck? Why is [unclear 00:38:51] revenue down so much? I thought we were busy down there. So Hilary investigates and says, "Yes, you're right that we're above budget and volume and several hundred thousand dollars below budget and revenue. Something's up." Well, three or four years ago, we didn't have Kevin to go and investigate. Well, now we do, along with Hilary and Ted, and 45 days later it's fixed. What does that mean to you? Well, two months ago, we had a revenue of 12.7 and that was below where we need to be, and we were starting to fret a little bit. This month, it's going to be right around 40 million, which from the perspective of operating the organization that you want to stop right now, that makes all the difference in the world, and it's because of all of these people doing their critically important roles better that we did them several years ago. I think the board meeting is a great opportunity to say, ride on, you know, awesome job.

Jill Buhler: [00:39:59] Absolutely.

Hilary Whittington: [00:40:02] There's a second layer to that. I don't know that this is the right place to mention it, but the hospital wasn't fantastic at succession planning, it really hasn't been. If we think of, you know, someone would leave radiology and have no idea like, what do we do? But we have these people who are excited to share the information, and there will be cool stories for all of you to know about the hard work that's going on behind the scenes [unclear 00:40:21] reports, monitoring reports, so it would just be like, "Here are hot things going on in the laboratory," or whatever it is, it's interesting information, but it gives those folks who are kind of the up-and-comers an opportunity to share what's going on in their departments, which keeps them --

Marie Dressler: [00:40:38] Motivated.

Hilary Whittington: [00:40:38] -- keeps them motivated, it keeps them excited, but it also keeps them increasing their professional exposure, which leaves us in the position where we're not stumped of what to do if, you know, if Joyce can't give the presentation, who would give it for her? We cancel the presentation is what we do, and if we're in a mode where we have more folks running the hospital who interact with you, then you can get information whenever you need.

Mike Glenn: [00:41:03] Good point.

Marie Dressler: [00:41:05] And it's a different perspective too, if it's a different person. So in the same department, it's a different perspective, and not everybody obviously sees things the same way, and I think that would be certainly more informative.

Jill Buhler: [00:41:17] Well, it makes them feel like we care, and we value what they're doing.

Marie Dressler: [00:41:21] Well, and from the staff point of view, yes, but also it informs us from a different perspective how we're taking care of our patients and families. The bottom line is, as far as I'm concerned, if we focus on patient care and provision of services to a standard, not just an adequate standard, a standard that is [unclear 00:41:47] hospital. That's what's important to me for my constituents. We've got to keep the hospital doing what it's doing now, solvent, increasing in our abilities to provide services, to take care of our patients to the highest quality and safest manner, and in some ways I don't care how it's, I mean, legally obviously done --

[Laughter]

Marie Dressler: -- but done to the best ability and that we, as the board, can see that it's happening. That's really all that I care about.

Matt Ready: [00:42:28] I have a question. Do we think the job of the board is define the ends of the organization? Define the purpose in what the goals for Mike are?

Jill Buhler: [00:42:38] I don't understand.

Matt Ready: [00:42:41] This is policy governance terminology, the global ends; it's the job of the board to define, *this is what we want you to do*. Is that our job?

[Crosstalk]

Tony Deleo: [00:42:50] I think it's a job for us to sit down with Mike and do that around the cable.

Jill Buhler: [00:42:53] Yeah.

Marie Dressler: [00:42:56] Like we're doing now.

Tony Deleo: [00:42:58] If you want to go and get a degree in healthcare administration and be able to have your toes in enough puddles to understand and decide where we should go, but if we take what our grasp of our community and its needs, and meld that together with Mike's knowledge of the operation of the hospital, and the industry, we can come up with some really cool stuff. But if we try to create that in a vacuum, it's going to be crap.

Chuck Russell: [00:43:27] None of us would be Commissioners if we didn't realize the importance of the hospital in this community.

Matt Ready: [00:43:32] That's not what I said. Is it our job to define his goals? Is that our -- I mean, we can do it with collaboration, we can obviously say, "Mike, if you think some of these goals are stupid or bad, absolutely tell us," but I think it's the board's job to ultimately agree *these are the goals*, and then the moat, Mike crosses the moat and he goes and achieves the goals and we could refine how we monitor that, but is it a board job to define the goals of the organization?

Marie Dressler: [00:44:05] I don't -- I actually agree to some degree with Matt on that. I think it is our job to agree with goals, but I think because he's the one who's trained, educated, experienced, knowledgeable, about these issues, he is the one who knows where the trends are going, brings them to us and we then evaluate, do our jobs, research, and see if he's going off on a complete tangent, which is going to lead us down the tubes or nowhere. Or, as he's been doing, is getting us ahead of the game and taking care of our communities.

Jill Buhler: [00:44:41] And I think it depends on what level of goals you're looking at. I mean, are you talking about the end goal? Or are you talking about the days of cash on hand or --

Matt Ready: [00:44:56] I'm talking about global ends. The end goals of the organization. If that's our job, and I think it is, I don't think we've ever really done it. I think we started it, I don't think we ever really got it into a level that was meaningful. It is still very high level, so basically, without that --

Jill Buhler: [00:45:23] It's because it's policy governance.

Matt Ready: [00:45:17] No. It's 'cause we didn't finish the work. It's because we didn't finish the work of actually defining the goals.

Jill Buhler: [00:45:23] No, because policy governance doesn't define the goal, it sets the goals. That's it.

Matt Ready: [00:45:28] You dig it, in police governance, you go down to whatever level of detail you feel is appropriate for the board to go to until they stop. You go down to measurable metrics. We never did that, so without actually giving Mike clear goals, we are not giving him goals, we are not really governing if we don't give him goals. We are just having faith that the goals that Mike comes to us and says, "This is what I'm going to accomplish," right, a strategic plan, and luckily, I think it's great Mike is really good, he's very talented and he's done some great strategic plans, and he puts some solid metrics in, but he's not responding to governance in my opinion. He is, in my opinion, 'cos I don't think he needed to look at these ends and figure out the strategic plan, there's not much here. I mean it just basically says, provide healthcare services. Within that, he can do whatever he feels is best. So we can throw our policy governance out, but I'm still going to say, it's our job to define the goals of the organization, and until we do that, in a meaningful specific way, I don't think we're really governing. We are riding the boat that Mike is, that our CEO, whoever happens to be our CEO at the time is, is driving.

Jill Buhler: [00:46:59] Well it sounds like you have some specific goal type things that you're thinking about. It would be helpful, to me at least, if you could say what -- go a little further with your explanation or your question, because I'm not quite getting at what level you're talking about.

Matt Ready: [00:47:24] Well, that would be an ends exercise. I mean, we went through this process of defining these three ends, with the one high level ends, and I think you dig it down a little bit further and, you know, that's the --

Chuck Russell: [00:47:47] Specific goals in a job with this kind of breadth are pretty hard to come up with. We have the responsibility, if Mike starts doing really weird stuff, we can't even hire another one, and State Law spells that out. It's our primary responsibility to hire and fire the CEO.

Tony Deleo: [00:48:05] If I may --

Chuck Russell: [00:48:06] But to specifically say, on Tuesday's Mike should always check the garbage or something...

[Laughter]

Chuck Russell: [00:48:11] You don't do that.

Jill Buhler: [00:48:11] Oh! There's one! [Laughs]

Matt Ready: [00:48:14] No, that would be too specific. I mean, potentially, one that would fit perfect, you know, we say, residents have access to superior quality healthcare services, so I believe you could get a little bit more specific in the quality realm --

Marie Dressler: [00:48:30] So give us an example.

Jill Buhler: [00:48:33] Yeah.

Marie Dressler: [00:48:33] Give us a couple of three examples, say if we have three metrics on that one.

Tony Deleo: [00:48:38] But in Carver , the thing they drilled into our heads for five days straight with cold showers --

[Laughter]

Tony Deleo: [00:48:45] -- was that you want to stand with the biggest bowl you can. If you can't do the job with the biggest bowl, you go to the next [unclear 00:48:53] and the next model which is getting more and more into detail. And what that is, that's a big bowl that everything fits into, that one statement, and if I may just take off on one of my tangents, so bare with me, is the omelette analogy. The omelette analogy is simply this. How are you going to judge a good omelette? You can judge it by watching the guy making the omelette to make sure he whisks it 34 times counterclockwise in an 3/4 bowl, and if he does all that, it's a good omelette. Or, you can tell him, "Make me an omelette," he does it, doesn't care how he does it, he puts it in front of you, and it tastes good. To me, what I want is a good tasting omelette. I don't care what the hell he mixes it with, as long as it comes out with the end product which is a good edible omelette.

If we get to counting how many times Mike is turning the whisk, and focus so much on that that we forget to come out here and see the quality of the omelette, then we're not doing our job, 'cos what we want, we don't want to do this, this, and -- all this micro-crap, excuse me in the middle, all we want is the people that come to our hospital to have healthcare. They have good healthcare, they go in sick, they come out alive and better. We want people who want to come to our hospital because they're going to get good care by people who care about them. We are an organization that is dedicated to making our community healthier in so many ways, in reaching out and working with other agencies. That's my omelette, and I'll tell you, to me it tastes pretty good. That's just me.

Jill Buhler: [00:50:38] Then there are ways to measure the quality indicators, there are all kinds of things that are out there that we can use to say how good is the quality that we have. We're being measured that way.

Mike Glenn: [00:50:52] Plus, I think that access to care is probably a goal on most people's strategic plans. It's possible that there might be seven definitions of access to care just in this room right now, but I know there'd be more than one. So last year, our main metric in access to care was optimized Medicaid expansion, get out there, 'cos that is the program in this State, a way in which we can improve access to care by giving people insurance they didn't have the day before. So that was the focus, and that focus was more external, you know, let's [unclear 00:51:46] widen it out and improve access to people, let's give access to people outside the system that didn't have it before. So we monitored that and it's something that we talked a lot about in SLG, and Hilary and Aaron, and several other people partnered with public health and executed on that. This year's access to care goal is more about the primary care network, and the whole [Cullman] initiative is, let's find a model that we think is better for providers, patients, and system, and let's measure that by reduce third available appointment to five days or less. That is the best, community wide for people inside this system, measure of access that's out there. Basically, it's the quantity to measure, not the quality of measure of do you have enough providers or not., and we've -- prior to us focusing on that, it was just this qualitative measure and the first time we tried to wrap our arms around it is when we did the data that -- the utilization and capacity study when [Carey Day] left, that determined that our [unclear 00:53:17] physician was providing of seeing 12 patients a day, and well, we got that up to 14. That's like adding two and a half providers, and we got that to 16, that's like adding five providers. Maybe we should look at internal capacity, and so Cullman was a tool to help get us to find that internal capacity. So this year's focus is people within the system, and Sara Smiths, she used to be like 60 days out and now she's like 15 days. If we execute on that, we will improve that definition of access to care. Well, it's my hunch that in the next year or so there will -- either we identify another high priority community need, internal or external with respect to access to care, or, and after spending the last two days here, what becomes clear to me is that it's not -- we're going to have to identify and find our own problems or challenges at stake, or the federal government's going to do it for us. This whole accountable community of health [unclear 00:54:40] dramatic shakeup and no one really knows what exactly it's going to look like, and this is going to go live the next year, 2016.

Marie Dressler: [00:54:50] In six months.

Mike Glenn: [00:54:52] So I'm thinking, sort of trying to [inaudible] how does this fit, and trying to determine the role of the board, board and governance, the goal should be accessed care, we should work on accessed care [crosstalk] but I do think the best practice might be for administrations to say [unclear 00:55:17], this is what we see, and here's the data to support it, but this is what I think we should work on right now.

Jill Buhler: [00:55:25] Yes, because we fetter, we fetter you if we try to define what that means, because it means different things at different times, access to care, you just heard two different things, there's more coming down the line, so we have to be -- we don't have the foresight, the knowledge, the expertise to define what access to care means. That's why we rely on, Mike.

Marie Dressler: [00:55:53] That's why he's hired. That's why we have a CEO [crosstalk].

Mike Glenn: [00:55:57] But ultimately, you have the ability to reject it, and this is coming from the perspective of what's the best answer, what's the right answer that balances the board owning the metric, and owning setting administrations, goals and priorities, but also administration may be having more on the ground expertise as to what's around the corner or what we are seeing, and so therefore this is what think we need the most pressing access to care issue. Next year it might be behavioral health. Maybe after we implement Dr. Ulrich, we discover that, holy smokes, that's just a finger in the dike and now that we've got this model that can be we scaled up, that should be the focus. So how do you develop a governing structure that sort of allows for that, that covers this landscape of here are the five or six things that are most important and here's how from a [yearlier], every other year basis we provide some definition to that and accountability metrics to determine whether [why they were cheating it or not].

Matt Ready: [00:57:22] So we have one of our ends, residents have access to superior quality healthcare services, so what does that mean? Can you conceive of anything -- under what scenario would you say, "Mike, you didn't do that?" What would he have to do for us to say, "Mike, you've failed to achieve residents have access to superior quality services"?

Jill Buhler: [00:57:47] If quality scores were dropping.

Matt Ready: [00:57:48] Yes, but at what point? When? How far do they have to drop before we say you haven't, you know [crosstalk].

Jill Buhler: [00:57:56] If they don't have an explanation, I mean if it starts to drop, that doesn't necessarily mean that we're going down [unclear 00:58:06], that could mean that there needs to be an explanation of what's happening and trend, they're looking at trends, you're always looking at trends, and if there isn't a satisfactory answer, and then you keep your eye on it, and then your other indicators have gone down and your DNV is --

Matt Ready: [00:58:28] I'm just saying, if you tell your school Superintendent that your job is teach kids and there is no agree criteria for how he could possibly do that, you have a meaningless criteria. It doesn't say anything. We have -- residents have access to superior quality healthcare services, I mean, you know what Mike? People don't have access to dental care. Well, that violates this, but you know what? We all agree, we don't provide dental care services. I mean there should be a little bit more specificity what this means. What is superior quality? Do you say, "We want to be at the 75th percentile industry standard metrics. You figure out what those are."

Chuck Russell: [00:59:10] We have everybody and their little brother coming by and inspecting us every year.

Tony Deleo: [00:59:13] That is why we participate in all the surveys that we do. This is comparing us against the national yardstick.

Matt Ready: [00:59:19] Right. And what would have to happen to say, "You've failed in quality?" What possible -- just 'cos they've gone down, I mean, we've seen quality scores going down, we never say, "Mike, you're failing to achieve this end," because there's no argument a board member could say -- unless they really got bad, Mike would have to -- the place would have to have quality scores plummeting I think, and we might have board consensus that, okay, something's really is going wrong here, but as it is here, this is a virtually meaningless statement. It basically says, *do healthcare*, which is not governance, that is like, do healthcare and come back and tell us what you think that means, we're going to trust your education and trust your instincts and if it doesn't feel right then we'll say something, but we have nothing written, we haven't agreed what --

Mike Glenn: [01:00:16] I don't disagree. I think that's bogus too. But I think it's -- we've got a mission, we've got a vision, value statements and a strategic plan. I don't really -- and now we have this. It's another body of work that in my mind -- so all the organizations that don't employ policy governance, which the other 37 public hospital districts that this is, these are their global ends, it's like, what's your vision? And if you look at our vision statement that Jefferson Healthcare will be the community's first choice for quality healthcare by providing exceptional patient care to every person we serve, you might say, well sure, this is a longer version of that, but delivering the safest highest quality of care of any healthcare organization or region, providing leadership to improve the health, wellness and vitality of our community, champion and engage workforce, demonstrating physical stewardship and thoughtful decision making, that that's it. That is it. That's -- and I do sit in your chair, I mean, I am able to go from operations to governance. That to me is what you would want, that is our reason to be, and if it's not, change it; but that's the mission and the vision of the organization, that's the higher overarching global end. We exist to together meet the needs of our community, and I think to the extent, to the detail that you think is appropriate, you can [tack] on to the mission, vision and values, and it comes out in the strategic plan and ultimately in the report card. [Unclear 01:02:31] when we were putting the first strategic plan together we spent some time trying to figure out how all of this stuff was connected, and when we were creating it, 'cos it's all relatively new, we spent a lot of time with that, you know, the triangle, and the performance improvement methodology was at the base, and driving all of this stuff, to me the policy governance stuff is just how we've sort of been out there and it's as meaningless to me as it is to you.

Jill Buhler: [01:03:10] That's exactly what one of the reasons policy governance doesn't work. We spend a lot of time, we spent a whole day in Atlanta coming up with an end, and that was basically it, it was a little shorter than that even, and that is under Carter, that's the end, that was the -- so that's part of what's the problem with policy governance.

Matt Ready: [01:03:36] This is the board saying what the goal is. It's like the owner of a sports team says to the coach and the general manager, I want a team that's in the play-offs every year and I expect you to win the championship at least once every five years. That's global ends. This is the playbook, the general manager, you are now -- you have to make the playbook, this is the detailed playbook that I agree, the board is actually not qualified to nitpick the metrics in the strategic plan.

Mike Glenn: [01:04:09] The strategic plan Matt, or a vision? 'Cos I would say the vision is the overarching --

Matt Ready: [01:04:14] I say the mission and vision, although we didn't' draft that, right, you drafted that with C-Suite, and that should be a -- that should align really nicely with the board's stated goals, which are going to be a mission statement, often is a little more flowery 'cos it's also sort of part marketing material, but the ends is the board trying to just say really clearly this is your job, this is what we want to achieve with the appropriate level of detail, and then hopefully then the mission and vision you come up with will align nicely with the board. In this case, we might need to, if we were going to refine this, we might look at the mission and vision and we might reverse-engineer it a little bit to make this, to flush this out, if we'd actually ever got to the work of defining the board goals.

Mike Glenn: [01:05:14] The mission -- the board has to own the mission and vision, whether we drafted it, because that's the most practical way to -- you were part of that painful process, which was more painful than the exercises on home health that you guys sat through, but that's the board's -- you ultimately have to say yes, that's who we are, and if what we came up with was way off the mark, well then send us back to do it again, or take it on yourself.

Matt Ready: [01:05:51] You see, I disagree. I think this is what the board has to own at this level, and once we do this work, once we do this work where we have our goals and we have it clear, then when you do the work on the mission it'll be a much easier exercise to see if this aligns, you know, this looks like, yeah, you have a good plan to achieve board goals.

Mike Glenn: [01:06:10] So 37 public hospital districts

accomplish what you are describing in some level of success or another without that.

Jill Buhler: [01:06:24] Yes, without policy governance.

Mike Glenn: [01:06:25] And it's the -- in the two or three organizations, it's the strat- it's the mission and the vision, you know, this is who we are, this is what we're about, and some missions are flowery, others aren't, but at the vision statement, then if you look at the vision statement you can hang a lot of -- it's open to different types of interpretation about access to care, what does that mean, reaching out to the community --

Matt Ready: [01:06:56] Did the board vote on the vision? Mission and vision sentiment?

Mike Glenn: [01:06:58] Yes, the board was involved in --

Matt Ready: [01:07:00] But did we actually vote and approve it as a mission vision...?

Marie Dressler: [01:07:02] I think we did.

Mike Glenn: [01:07:03] Absolutely.

Chuck Russell: [01:07:05] I'm sure we did.

Mike Glenn: [01:07:05] Absolutely, and there were check-ins and so it was a more collegial exercise, or participative exercise than I think you're giving it credit for. It wasn't administration, you know, "show up on a Wednesday I've to another thing for you to approve."

Matt Ready: [01:07:21] I know I spent like two special sessions working with the board members on this. I don't know that we spent that level of attention on the mission vision. It was more like the strategic plan. I don't actually remember a separate discussion on mission and vision, and I don't know that we even have, we don't have any sort of policy where -- in policy governance you check in every year and the policy [unclear 01:07:48] affirm, do we have a policy on mission and vision? Is that brought before the board every year?

Jill Buhler: [01:07:51] Probably not because we've been working on this.

Tony Deleo: [01:07:55] You often taken all the time on the process and not spending it on the product.

Jill Buhler: [01:08:00] That's exactly right.

Tony Deleo: [01:08:00] That's the problem. And if I may, I'm going to extend a little bit on your thing about the team. You're telling the coach, "I want the playoffs every five years," and this and this; now to me, if I was the owner, I'd be telling the coach, "Make me money. I bought the team for $10 million, I want a million dollars a year at the end, I don't care what the hell you do, I want that million dollars a year over my investment."

Matt Ready: [01:08:25] That's right, so that is why you have different vote plans, we have to agree on this.

Tony Deleo: [01:08:29] But it doesn't tell Mike that he needs to be in the playoffs every five years and he needs to be winning 60% of his game.

Matt Ready: [01:08:36] So if we were five owners of this team, we'd be having this debate; what's more important, making money or being in the playoffs, and we would argue about this and we would define that and we'd give it to him. We would not argue about his playbook. We would say, "Okay, we want you to make us at least a half million dollars a year and we want to be in the playoffs at least every other year. We would come to some agreement and then he would know --

Tony Deleo: [01:08:56] He could have the world's worst team ever to hit the gridiron, but if he has an incredible marketing plan, he's going to make me money from selling hats and T-shirts.

Matt Ready: [01:09:09] Yes, he could be the LA Clippers and that's how they do it.

Tony Deleo: [01:09:12] So there we go. Let the man who knows what he's doing do his job and we give him the general parameters, which is make money on the football team or provide exceptional healthcare to our community, and as long as he's accomplishing that, great.

Matt Ready: [01:09:32] I agree, I just don't think we really -- we're not going the general parameters in a meaningful way. If you want to throw out ends and we start treating mission and vision as the board's definition of what his goals are, then I would say we need to immediately discuss what's our process, our annual process for reviewing mission and vision, and how are we going to approve to it, because it's basically going to become this, and I think we're going to need a more rigorous process in how we define that, and how we judge it, and what makes it meaningful and useful for the board as a governing instrument.

Tony Deleo: [Unclear 01:10:12] accumulative at the survey, accumulatively at our certifications, at the state orders, reports, and if all of those things are in line, if we don't have a huge backlog of patient complaints through our patient advocate, I mean just the basic parameters.

Matt Ready: [01:10:31] You're just rattling off what you think should be the criteria, I mean, that's a discussion the board should have and say, "These are the things that we -- how we monitor your performance, these are the things that are meaningful to us."

Jill Buhler: [01:10:58] So basically, you don't really care much about actual policy governance as much as you do establishing the goal.

Matt Ready: [01:11:12] That's just one, and to me that's the most important aspect that policy governance gives us a nice structure for how the board defines the goals of the organization, I think it defines a nice structure for how you monitor other things the board's supposed to monitor, but it sounds like everyone's like wants to throw the whole thing out so I decided to focus in on a very specific piece. How about the steering wheel? Does everyone agree we need a steering wheel in the boat? And that the board is in charge of picking out the destination for the boat? So instead of saying, we shouldn't have a freighter or something --

Tony Deleo: [01:11:52] Do we need a boat? If we're going to get from point A to point B, maybe a floatplane is a whole lot more efficient.

Matt Ready: [01:11:59] Yes, and it might just be choosing the destination. Are we going to Hawaii or are we going to Cancun? It might just be that.

Tony Deleo: [01:12:05] That kind of sounds like our mission and vision and values.

Matt Ready: [01:12:09] It could be.

Tony Deleo: [01:12:10] And Mike's the one that figures out whether we go by sailboat or by floatplane. Madam Chairman, may I ask for a two-minute recess?

Jill Buhler: [01:12:18] Yes.

Tony Deleo: [01:12:18] Thank you. Okay, we all need to stretch out --

Matt Ready: [01:12:20] Are we in recess?

Jill Buhler: [01:12:21] Yes.

[Recess]

Jill Buhler: [01:12:26] Now, from our break, where were we?

Mike Glenn: [01:12:32] It seems to me the discussion was testing, is policy governance best way to govern Jefferson Healthcare? And there are some folks on the governance side of the table and the operation side of the table that believe it may not be. So there's been good dialogue about that, and I think ultimately the board needs to continue to discuss this and at a regular session retake up the issue and decide if we want to go in a different direction --

Jill Buhler: [01:13:18] How about if I or anybody who wants to, kind of investigates other models out there. No need to reinvent the wheel. That way we could maybe have a framework, something that we could look at that might be working better. Find some effective boards.

Matt Ready: [01:13:47] Yes, I think that makes more sense if someone came in with a proposed framework rather than, "Oh, we're just not going to do --

Jill Buhler: [01:13:55] Oh, yeah.

Matt Ready: [01:13:55] -- just throw out our current method of governance," and not have --

Tony Deleo: [01:13:58] [Inaudible]

Matt Ready: [01:13:59] -- yeah, but come in with, *this is the basic framework of how the board's going to govern the hospital district.*

Jill Buhler: [01:14:09] Yeah. Okay.

Tony Deleo: [01:14:09] I'll see what I come up with and then I'll ship it up to you when I get it.

Jill Buhler: [01:14:13] Great.

Mike Glenn: [01:14:14] I could reach out to other organizations, just get your --

Jill Buhler: [01:14:19] School boards, they're kind of like us.

Mike Glenn: [01:14:21] That's like public hospital districts.

Jill Buhler: [01:14:22] Yeah.

Mike Glenn: [01:14:23] 'Cos I do think that there are some -- I think Kittitas has --

Marie Dressler: [01:14:27] I was going to say, who would you --

Mike Glenn: [01:14:28] They seem to do a pretty darn good job.

Marie Dressler: [01:14:30] -- who would you suggest? Or even the talk from yesterday.

Mike Glenn: [01:14:36] It's not a public hospital.

Marie Dressler: [01:14:37] Oh, it's not -- oh, no, that's right, they're private. Yes.

Matt Ready: [01:14:40] If only we had a conference where representatives from these hospitals would all be in one place and we could like --

Jill Buhler: [01:14:45] Wouldn't that be nice?

Matt Ready: [01:14:45] -- each just grab people and talk to them.

Jill Buhler: [01:14:48] That would be nice.

Marie Dressler: [01:14:49] Or maybe we should ask WSHA put something like that on at a subsequent meeting, 'cos we're not the only board that has issues with governance and other issues.

Mike Glenn: [01:15:00] It may not surprise you to learn that governance is a topic in most WSHA administrative means.

Matt Ready: [01:15:06] So you said Kittitas.

Mike Glenn: [01:15:09] Yeah, Elbert.

Matt Ready: [01:15:12] Any others like off the top of our heads that we think are like the most amazing performing public hospital districts that we might use as our best practice, go to people to talk to?

Mike Glenn: [01:15:23] Pullman [unclear 01:15:26].

Jill Buhler: [01:15:29] Which one?

Hilary Whittington: [01:15:29] Pullman. I wonder if even just reaching out to [unclear 01:15:32] and asking him, because he presents other's boards, I mean all of their clients.

Jill Buhler: [01:15:37] Could you do that?

Hilary Whittington: [01:15:37] Sure.

Jill Buhler: [01:15:38] Oh, great.

Matt Ready: [01:15:40] What if we'd actually liked one of these districts, what if we invited them to come and do a little presentation, *this is how it works*, you know, and gave us sort of a model to look at and ask questions of --

Jill Buhler: [01:15:56] Yeah, great idea. Great idea.

Marie Dressler: [01:15:56] Can you [crosstalk] or maybe two people could do a field trip to their meeting. Just sit down and watch it.

Jill Buhler: [01:16:01] Yeah, that would be [crosstalk].

Matt Ready: [01:16:03] I would do that.

Mike Glenn: [01:16:04] Olympic?

Jill Buhler: [01:16:06] Yeah, Olympic, they seem to be good.

Mike Glenn: [01:16:06] An hour away, maybe a start by going and watching them do their business. What has happened in the move to policy governance and I also think a past board member deciding to widen the screen as opposed to tighten the screen of what's presented, if you look at the agenda of Olympic Medical Center, click, click, click... all kind of items, physician contracts...

Jill Buhler: [01:16:33] Wow.

Mike Glenn: [01:16:37] I don't know if it's their -- some of it is the board's bylaws and how they do business, but some of it also is just the culture, the expectation, this is what we expect to hear, but we frequently get poked at by the press that when we send out our board agenda they're like, "Well, what? Really? What else? There's twelve things on this," well, no there's only four or five things, so it would be interesting to go and check out a few to see if that makes sense or not. You know, the county, ever see the county? Every $5 thousand MOU with the Sanitation Department they'll vote on.

Chuck Russell: [01:17:26] So the press wants more detail on our agenda.

Mike Glenn: [01:17:29] Well, because they want to have -- on Sundays they have a public meeting section and the five or six different public agencies and they like to write a little blurb about it. So the more stuff that we identify the more filler for their article. I think it's just that, public information, here's what's going on in your public agencies.

Jill Buhler: [01:17:56] It's great.

Tony Deleo: [01:17:57] If I might suggest, if we're going to get policies from other agencies, either one person do that or we split it up, you know, two or three so we're not going to do it sending a duplicate request.

Jill Buhler: [01:18:10] Two different people, yeah. That's a good idea. So Hilary, you're going to talk to Tom for his ideas, okay. I know Joan at Kittitas I can talk to her.

Marie Dressler: [01:18:26] Tom Martin? No, who's the --

Mike Glenn: [01:18:30] At Pullman Scott.

Marie Dressler: [01:18:31] Scott.

Chuck Russell: [01:18:33] If we all go to somebody else's meeting, then are we meeting?

Jill Buhler: [01:18:38] Yeah.

Marie Dressler: [01:18:38] We don't all have to go, just two people can go. Otherwise, it's a meeting.

Tony Deleo: [01:18:44] Unless it's considered educational.

Marie Dressler: [01:18:45] Well, if we don't discuss the district's business it could be termed that.

Matt Ready: [01:18:51] I think the most we'd learn from [being able to] -- I'd just ask direct questions to a board member and/or CEO. That's where we'd really get a feel for how it works. A board meeting would give us little bit of a feel.

Marie Dressler: [01:19:07] I think you need to do both, because there's a different level of interest and activity with all board members. If you have a five or seven member board, then there'll be different levels of, if you like, education, knowledge, interest, some people don't say much, other people say too much, a few have no idea of what's going on, and other people are so glued in they could run the hospital themselves.

Jill Buhler: [01:19:35] What about Ben?

Mike Glenn: [01:19:37] Where?

Marie Dressler: [01:19:37] Ben, WSHA.

Mike Glenn: [01:19:39] Oh, Ben. [Unclear 01:19:40]

Jill Buhler: [01:19:42] He's pretty inundated though, isn't he? Maybe he probably wouldn't want to -- I wonder if there's any resource there though?

Mike Glenn: [01:19:51] There's a growing body of work about governance performance going on in WSHA right now.

Marie Dressler: [01:19:58] Good. So we're ahead of that game too.

Jill Buhler: [01:20:03] Who would be a contact?

Mike Glenn: [01:20:04] [Priven] because of the significant difference between public hospital district governance and non public hospital district governance.

Tony Deleo: [01:20:14] I can touch base with MRSC, they have some sample policies.

Jill Buhler: [01:20:18] Okay, you do the MRSC, I'll talk to Ben and Joan. Anybody wants to talk to anybody else?

Tony Deleo: [01:20:30] Mike, you want to talk to Eric about [crosstalk].

Mike Glenn: [01:20:31] Yeah, yeah. I'm happy to get Olympic Sport bylaws and --

Marie Dressler: [01:20:36] And Scott [unclear 01:20:36]?

Mike Glenn: [01:20:37] Yep.

Marie Dressler: [01:20:39] Didn't he -- do you want paper?

Mike Glenn: [01:20:48] No, got it.

Jill Buhler: [01:20:50] Okay, so then we'll resume this conversation after we get some more information, right?

Marie Dressler: [01:21:00] Sounds like a plan.

Mike Glenn: [01:21:02] An advantage of starting this discussion in June is that if we wanted to make a change, we have time to do in January 1.

Jill Buhler: [01:21:16] Yeah.

Mike Glenn: [01:21:21] Providing we move along.

Jill Buhler: [01:21:21] Can you think of any place that might, you might like to look at?

Marie Dressler: [01:21:25] Well, what about Univ-

Matt Ready: [01:21:29] I don't know other hospital districts that well.

Marie Dressler: [01:21:33] And what about Whidbey's got a new CEO, haven't they?

Mike Glenn: [01:21:38] I wouldn't, I would not --

Marie Dressler: [01:21:39] Yeah, I think, yeah, too --

Mike Glenn: [01:21:40] I think that's -- because what is clear is that board, for a lack of a better word, dysfunction is a drag on organization performance. It's not really easy to make a smaller hospital perform at a okay to high level, so that's why there's discussion going on at WSHA. How many of these little hospitals are struggling because of --

Marie Dressler: [01:22:16] Board dysfunction. That's bad news for our patients, that's for sure.

Chuck Russell: [01:22:23] I forget, did we have enabling legislation to -- did we probably vote for policy governance at one point?

Jill Buhler: [01:22:32] Oh yeah, we did.

Marie Dressler: [01:22:33] Yes.

Chuck Russell: [01:22:35] Right after we got back from the great expedition.

Jill Buhler: [01:22:40] So what time is it?

Mike Glenn: [01:22:41] One o'clock.

Jill Buhler: [01:22:42] Okay, so now we could talk about what we learned.

Mike Glenn: [01:22:47] All right.

Jill Buhler: [01:22:51] [Laughs] Don't everybody talk at once.

Chuck Russell: [01:22:56] Well, I learned that my wife is going to remodel our fishing cabinets and I'm going to get copper handles on.

[Laughter]

Marie Dressler: [01:23:08] Now you know why we're [unclear 01:23:08].

Mike Glenn: [01:23:09] What has been reinforced is, Accountable Communities of Health and a couple of meetings ago, when we were talking about the role the hospital should play in our Community Health Improvement Plan and which I think everyone agrees sum - - the question is, you know, lead on participate, and the greater context of my consternation is if I'm not truly engaged, understanding, and leading this pretty nebulous exercise of understanding tapping into our Accountable Communities Of Health, no one's doing it. It's kind of one of those deals where, beginning of the year, I understood what the acronym was, so I was ahead of the curve.

On April 15, I attended a rural Hospital Committee and Claudia and all these WSHA people are grabbing a handful of us and saying, "Are you paying attention to this? Do you know that Kitsap Mental Health is the backbone agency? What's going on in Jefferson and [unclear 01:24:38] because Kitsap's organizing and what are you doing?" So exponential leap, and then two months later, another exponential leap in importance and smoke beginning to clear, and that's not where my head is right now. I mean I'm keeping that plate spinning but in 2016 your governance policies for the Accountable Communities Of Health, in order for you to be designated one, have to be complete, and think about this discussion going on, governance, right? where a bunch of organizations that haven't necessarily been on the top of the dollar food chain, by virtue of them [laughs] sitting around this very small table, are developing policies on where this big river of resources is going to come.

So that has to be my focus. I have to figure that out, and what's our role, and so the great thing about Jefferson Count- 'cos what's going on in other counties is the other organizations are swinging their elbows at the hospital, but they're saying it's a great comeuppance, that, you know, it's no longer hospital-centric, and so we're going just fine and you can have a seat at the table but we already have these big seats. In Jefferson County, Gene Baldwin has been awesome, Tom Lock has been awesome, Adam Marques has been awesome, so we are tag-teaming this, and Gene we've meeting scheduled to talk about it, we met at Olympic, [David Salmon] from Forks, Eric and me, Tom and Gene, to chat about it we met at Kitsap or Silverdale with David Schultz, but I heard today that David Schultz from Harrison they might be --

Marie Dressler: [01:26:53] Moving him?

Mike Glenn: [01:26:53] -- opting out to Pierce.

Hilary Whittington: [01:26:55] Wow.

Jill Buhler: [01:26:56] What?

Mike Glenn: [01:26:57] Well, they would basically be on Franciscans.

Marie Dressler: [01:27:01] Yes, CHI.

Jill Buhler: [01:27:03] Well, where does that leave us? Because I thought we needed them to make it viable.

Mike Glenn: [01:27:06] Well, it complicates things.

Jill Buhler: [01:27:08] Yeah.

Mike Glenn: [01:27:09] But I'm not sure.

Jill Buhler: [01:27:10] Do we have the [Tribes]?

Mike Glenn: [01:27:12] [The Tribes] are figuring this out too. At some point, the nickel is going to drop. Someone's going to attend a seminar like we just attended, where two by four [upside the head] [laughs] this is a big deal, you know, the money's going to flow through -- 2016 they're going to have primary care and behavioral health, and it's better to be lucky than good, right? When we brought on Sue Ehrlich we weren't thinking to position ourselves for Accountable Community of Health, yeah, but that's it, that is the model that people are going to think we're so smart and we just sort of --

Speaker 8: [01:27:49] Sue's coming back in town, how can we make that happen?

Marie Dressler: [01:27:51] We tripped over.

Mike Glenn: [01:27:52] Yeah. But then that's just where it starts, and then it grows larger and larger and larger to the point where we could be taking on risk. So that has to be huge, I mean that's a very important goal that the hospital, that seven months ago we had no idea was even, you know...

Marie Dressler: [01:28:13] So what is this deal if Harrison does --

Mike Glenn: [01:28:16] I don't know. I don't know. I don't know how they can. I mean it's a -- they are the hospital -- I think what it, there is a couple of different ACOs. Harrison is going to play, Franciscans partnered with Providence for this mega ACO, and I think Harrison will play in that one, but right now ACOs are commercial and Medicare. I think that they will also have to play in this Accountable Communities Of Health to take care of Kitsap County patients, because that's where that money's going to flow through. So I think that organizations are positioning themselves to dip their ladle in all of these different buckets, and we're doing it more linearly because that's how smaller organizations do it.

Tony Deleo: [01:29:15] Mike, is all the funding kind of coming through the ACH?

Mike Glenn: [01:29:18] Funding is going to -- the thinking is the healthcare authority, what they're doing is shedding risk. Right now, the healthcare authority on this fee for service base is that they're kind of at risk, that the more people that get sick, and on Medicaid, and their costs are, ultimately the State healthcare authority takes on that risk. Well, three or five years from now, they're just going to say, "Hey, look, we'll give you $1,000 per member, you take care of all of their needs, which --

Marie Dressler: [01:29:50] But that includes everything.

Mike Glenn: [01:29:52] Yeah. [Crosstalk] That's where they're going. That's population health management, and they're just going to parcel that out. Initially it's just going to be, they're going to kind of lead us to that slowly by --

Marie Dressler: [Unclear 01:30:07] industry or is that coming up in 20?

Mike Glenn: [01:30:09] Probably, probably. That's the work that's being done now.

Matt Ready: [01:30:13] When they get to that point, are we still talking just Medicare and commercial or are we talking everyone?

Mike Glenn: [01:30:20] Well, I think that it's probably going to be this patchwork of acronyms, because our rural ACO will be Medicare, our Accountable Community Of

Health will be Medicaid, and on all healthcare authority patients, maybe we could work with Lynn Barr and spin off a commercial ACO, maybe we go sit at Providence's table, but there's just not -- when you think about -- Medicare requires no fewer than five, no more than ten thousand... [01:31:01]

June 2015 - Numerous Meetings between June 24, 2015 and June 29, 2016 – Audio available for most meetings, but not yet transcribed.

June 29, 2016 - Jefferson Healthcare Commission Meeting in Chelan, WA Transcript of Dialogue

{Recording begins}

Matt Ready: So... just so you know.

Tony Deleo: We're not going to record this meeting Matt.

Matt Ready: I'm recording it.

Tony Deleo: No you're not.

Marie Dressler: That's not our policy, is it?

Kees Kolff: Wait, is this an official meeting?

Marie Dressler: It's an official board meeting, but our policy states that we record when we're in our normal board situation, board meeting room at the hospital.

Kees Kolff: There's nothing that prohibits Matt from recording it.

Tony Deleo: Yes there is. It makes it official record.

Kees Kolff: There should be an official record if it's an official meeting.

Mike Glenn: Well, there is a legal opinion that recommends to not do this actually, but we talked about that. And you're right.

Kees Kolff: I guess that's before my times.

Mike Glenn: Yeah. [Crosstalk] just not being difficult.

Tony Deleo: Are you still recording?

Matt Ready: I'm recording the meeting.

Tony Deleo: Okay.

Commissioner Deleo pushed out his chair and stood quickly up from the table.

[Matt Ready's personal account of this moment in the meeting:

I was seated to his right with at least one person in between us, but nonetheless, I remember my surprise at his actions.

When someone is angry with you and they suddenly rise from the table, you don't know what will happen next. My brain immediately started evaluating possibilities. I must admit, my body experienced a shot of extra adrenaline instinctively, since I suppose at a primal level, I perceived some sort of violence towards me was possible.

I saw my recorder sitting on the table out in front of me and thought, "Is he going to grab at my recorder?" The possibility seemed plausible as I had imagined such things happening at previous debates about the recording of meetings. In fact, I had played through many scenarios in my mind before about Hospital security guards or even police being called into board meetings to stop me from recording. Many times I had mentally prepared myself for such confrontations and had long ago decided I would continue recording under all circumstances and simply see what levels of force might be used against me. Yet, on this day, I was not so mentally prepared as I had no reason to believe all the commissioners would suddenly try to stop the recording again- which they hadn't done for months.

So I look at my recorder and prepare myself to casually reach out and take hold of it if Commissioner Deleo makes a move in my direction. I was attempting not to flinch at his sudden rise from the table, as in moments like this, getting you to flinch in fear can be part of the goal of the person attempting to move you. In any case, Commissioner Deleo did not make any move in my direction, instead he stepped away from the table and walked briskly towards the door and said:]

Tony Deleo: See you guys later! Let me know if he turns it off.

[Commissioner Deleo exits the room.]

Jill Buhler: This is a little counterproductive. Do you really want to do this Matt? [Unclear 00:01:19]

Matt Ready: [Breathes deeply]

[Pause]

Jill Buhler: Yes? No?

Matt Ready: Sorry, my stress level is very high right now, so it's hard for me to speak. [Crosstalk] I did not expect a massive conflict over this again. I didn't think you guys would be surprised. I recorded last year's meeting [last year's annual meeting in Chelan, Wa], if you recall, so I've told you before, I cannot actually remember everything that is said at these meetings, and it's important to me that we take what we say here seriously, and we're held accountable for what we say here, and the only way to do that is to have an accurate record of these meetings, and so I record the meetings.

Jill Buhler: The point is that you being a Commissioner, it is different than a member of the public recording the meeting, and we have no official recording device here so we can't record it and have it be an actual official recording. That's a different [unclear 00:03:18]. I think we need to either adjourn or conclude or...

Kees Kolff: Could I ask [crosstalk]--

Marie Dressler: Point of order, that we do have a policy I believe, which says that we make official recordings when we are in our official board setting in the hospital, and I believe you are aware of that, so I do take exception to the recording, but nothing to hide. But I think it is not something that, you know, if we have these policies and you're, and rightly so, very keen on following policies, and then you go, you yourself, go an break one. I don't see what this is all about. I think it's just a barrier to try to work for our patients, for our community, personally.

Kees Kolff: I obviously haven't been involved in this kind of discussion before, so I'm as the new kid on the block, if you wouldn't mind, first of all, the policies that we just revised, I guess I must not have read that section carefully enough, does it say that we only record in official meetings? Or does it say that we record in official meetings. I mean I'm wondering, do the policies also say that we don't in this kind of setting? I mean I just -- and again, this it just a point of clarification, I don't --

Jill Buhler: The point of clarification is that when we go, for example, to legislature, we did not want to be bound to record what the legislatures were saying because they may not feel free to speak. So for that reason, and because it can be a logistics nightmare to have it and where we don't have control of the venue, we voted, and Matt voted for that as well, to not record anything other than the meetings that were held in our normal venue [crosstalk].

Kees Kolff: In that case I would need to just check to see, because there's a difference between --

Jill Buhler: You can check it if you have the board book, 'cos it's --

Kees Kolff: No, I'm just saying to me it is important whether the policy says that we will *only* record under certain situations or that we *will* record under certain situations, but if there's no prohibition [crosstalk] I'm concerned if I could --

Marie Dressler: It says we do not, if we're out of the hospital, we do not [crosstalk] because we are legally responsible,

Kees Kolff: If I could finish --

Marie Dressler: -- as the Secretary I'm legally responsible for ensuring that we have the official copy open for the public records, and that is what our attorney has said, and we -- because it's [unclear 00:06:30] as Jill has just said, we have difficulty, we don't have recording equipment, we can't inflict this on other people like in previous board meeting. So it was decided that we would only record when we're at our board meetings in our home base, and this is not our home base. Maybe we'd like it to be, but it's not. So therefore, this leaves the Hospital District open to prosecution and fines because of our inability to have an official recording which is archived for the benefit of the community.

Kees Kolff: Although my question wasn't answered, I appreciate your clarifying [crosstalk].

Mike Glenn: Well, there's no prohibition. I mean, anybody could record anything. It's just the Council said that you either -- you have -- if you're going to vote to record board meetings, because other many boards don't, [unclear 00:07:33] doesn't record their board meetings, then you do it in a way that's controlled by the organization with your equipment and your system, which is why we and Susie do what she does, because it becomes the official public record and recommended against a board member recording and because that is something other than the public record.

Jill Buhler: And that's -- we're trying to go by [unclear 00:08:02] attorney [unclear 00:08:03].

Kees Kolff: Because that's other than a public record, but if an individual Commissioner records that because of The Open Public Records Act, that recording *does* become an official recording? I guess I'm trying to --

Mike Glenn: Yes, the law doesn't distinguish you from a community member and a board member, that you might be thinking you recorded this as a community member but the law [sees it as] recording as board member in that capacity, so therefore it's subject to [crosstalk] --

Kees Kolff: So therefore, what Matt records is, quote,

discoverable through public records.

Jill Buhler: Yes.

Tony Deleo: [Crosstalk] discoverable [crosstalk] to comply with -- I'm sorry.

Mike Glenn: We have an obligation to recording.

Kees Kolff: To make it -- I'm sorry? You have an obligation to --

Mike Glenn: Because it is an official public record that the public entity isn't the steward of, so that is the problem the attorney points out you want to avoid. [Crosstalk].

Jill Buhler: And if something happened --

Kees Kolff: I'd appreciate -- I'd love to get some more information and maybe you can share with the other --

Jill Buhler: It's too bad you didn't study this before him.

Kees Kolff: May I finish speaking please?

Jill Buhler: Please.

Kees Kolff: I'd love to see the letter from the attorney that describes that, just so that I can understand that, and I don't.

Jill Buhler: We need to get the same attorney that told you that [conclude].

Tony Deleo: Madam Chairman, if I could make a motion that we forbid Commissioner Ready from recording this meeting.

?Mike Glenn: [Unclear 00:09:59]

?Jill Buhler: Is there a second?

[Crosstalk]

Tony Deleo: Well, Madam Chairman, what's your call?

Jill Buhler: I'm going to ask Matt again and try to explain that, again, the reason for this is that if a particular board member has what is considered an official document and something happens to that document that is in his or her possession and it is not the actual official document, even though it's -- still it's discoverable, we have no way to refute or if somebody did something with that or did something out of context, we would have no way to verify or validate.

Kees Kolff: [Unclear 00:11:10] I appreciate your clarification of that and if I might, Matt, would you be willing to not record this session here today? I'd love to study this situation further and maybe you and I can speak some other time about the importance or relevance of recording and then cover [unclear 00:11:37].

Matt Ready: No. I'm recording the meeting. If it is a record for the hospital we can do the exact same thing we did with all the other recordings I made, I just put it in the same directory on the hospital server with all the other recordings. I do not understand the resistance everyone in the room has to recording a public meeting like we do every one of them.

Tony Deleo: [Unclear 00:12:10] required with recording, we have the problem whether you're recording it in the appropriate manner so it complies with the Open Public Records Acts or it complies with the Washington State archival requirements for maintaining public documents. Marie, as Secretary of this Board, is responsible for the maintenance and archiving of all official records of this board, because you are [active] as a Commissioner, because you're recording it, that makes it a [unclear 00:12:38] official recording of the board, which means it [falls] under all these requirements. That is what I have a problem with.

Matt Ready: And all those requirements are met by the hospital just having a copy of the recording?

Tony Deleo: No, by having the original.

Matt Ready: Well, there is no original. It's a digital -- there's no original digital -- it's copied. The minute it's copied to the server off the recording device, it's not an original, it's a digital image.

Mike Glenn: Well, it's Council's recommendation. I think that we settled that discussion. The best practice is that this is to be avoided. This is not best practice. That was the recommendation and I think that's what we are applying, or trying to adhere to.

Jill Buhler: Yes.

Kees Kolff: Would it make a difference if this digital recording were made available to the Secretary right at this time? I mean, would that -- again, I'm exploring for some pie in the sky compromise and I'm trying to see if there's some way to bridge the gap with that, and I don't know if Matt would be willing to relinquish his digital recorder to the Secretary. Would that make a difference in the situation or not?

Tony Deleo: Well, yeah, if you're a [unclear 00:14:28] Commissioner who refuses to yield to the will of the board, that refuses to --

Jill Buhler: Follow policy.

Tony Deleo: -- follow the recommendations of the attorney that's --

Jill Buhler: And to follow policy.

Tony Deleo: And to adhere to the State of --

Jill Buhler: [Unclear 00:14:40].

Kees Kolff: [Crosstalk] Could I ask for the answer to my question?

Jill Buhler: [Unclear 00:14:46].

Kees Kolff: Could I ask for the answer to my question if it would make a difference to the rest of the Commissioners if the digital recording were made immediately available so that...? I can appreciate that that's not --

Jill Buhler: It does not, because --

Kees Kolff: -- [the way] you understand the policy.

Jill Buhler: -- it's not to me because it does not follow policy.

Kees Kolff: Okay.

Jill Buhler: And that policy was voted on by four, five of the people here [inaudible] endlessly because of [this board book].

Kees Kolff: In that case, I would like to make a motion to conclude.

Jill Buhler: Is there a second?

Tony Deleo: Second.

Jill Buhler: Discussion [on paper].

Tony Deleo: Mike, I apologize for this happening.

Mike Glenn: That's all right.

Tony Deleo: [Do you have a] program to present?

Mike Glenn: I'm just going to kind of point out the obvious that there are issues here.

Matt Ready: Have we -- I'll turn it off if we have officially concluded.

Jill Buhler: Yes.

Section 2: Compilations and Mashups

See Book 2 when published.